BEST

DAD

EVER

summersdale

BEST DAD EVER

Compiled by Mark Wright

An Hachette UK Company
www.hachette.co.uk

Summersdale Publishers Ltd
Part of Octopus Publishing Group Limited
Carmelite House
50 Victoria Embankment
LONDON
EC4Y 0DZ
UK

www.summersdale.com

Printed and bound in China

ISBN: 978-1-80007-023-3

Substantial discounts on bulk quantities of Summersdale books are available to corporations, professional associations and other organizations. For details contact general enquiries: telephone: +44 (0) 1243 771107 or email: enquiries@summersdale.com.

To.......................................

From.....................................

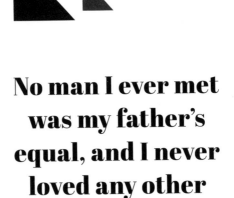

No man I ever met was my father's equal, and I never loved any other man as much.

Hedy Lamarr

"Father" is the
noblest title a
man can be given.

Robert L. Backman

YOU GIVE ME EVERYTHING: YOUR TIME, YOUR SUPPORT, AND YOUR LOVE

The impression made by a father's voice can set in motion an entire trend of life.

Gordon MacDonald

A father carries
pictures where
his money used
to be.

Anonymous

The greatest gift that I can give my children is the freedom to be who they are.

Will Smith

DADS
ARE
MAGIC

Moms should know that even the manliest guys will become softies when they have daughters.

Jimmy Fallon

We need to
show our kids
that you're
not strong by
putting other
people down –
you're strong by
lifting them up.

Barack Obama

I'M SO PROUD TO BE YOUR CHILD

We don't lose ourselves in parenthood. We find parts of ourselves we never knew existed.

L. R. Knost

Fatherhood didn't just happen to me. I am deliberately living it, re-imagining it, and rediscovering it every day.

Hrithik Roshan

My daughter and I speak about having the confidence to believe in your own journey and not to follow others.

Idris Elba

NO MATTER HOW TALL I GROW, I WILL ALWAYS LOOK UP TO YOU

THE OLDER I GET, THE SMARTER MY FATHER SEEMS TO GET.

Tim Russert

Fatherhood has changed me – it has to change you. It's not about your needs any more; it's about everyone else's.

Peter Kay

BEING A FATHER IS TOUGH, BUT YOU ALWAYS DO IT WITH A SMILE

My father taught me you have to believe in yourself and run on your own track.

Jennifer Grey

ANYONE WHO DOES ANYTHING TO HELP A CHILD IN HIS LIFE IS A HERO TO ME.

Fred Rogers

What do I owe
my father?
Everything.

Henry van Dyke

THANKS FOR BEING THE KIND OF PERSON I ASPIRE TO BE

When I was a kid
I used to imagine
animals running
under my bed.
I told my dad...
He cut the legs
off the bed.

Lou Brock

What matters is being a good father and a good husband – just being connected to family as much as possible.

David Beckham

ALL
THE TIMES
YOU THINK
I DON'T
NOTICE
THE LITTLE
THINGS –
I DO

Children
are a poor
man's riches.

English proverb

When you meet your kids you realize that they deserve great parents...
and you have to try and become the person that they deserve.

Ryan Gosling

I decided in my life
that I would do
nothing that did not
reflect positively
on my father's life.

Sidney Poitier

**NOT A DAY
GOES BY
WHERE
I DON'T
FEEL LUCKY
TO HAVE
A FATHER
LIKE YOU**

There's no one I'd rather be with than my kids.

Ralph Lauren

Dads are most ordinary men turned by love into heroes, adventurers, storytellers, and singers of song.

Pam Brown

YOU ARE
ALWAYS
MY ROCK

You don't raise heroes, you raise sons. And if you treat them like sons, they'll turn out to be heroes, even if it's just in your own eyes.

Walter Schirra Sr

Fathering is not something perfect men do, but something that perfects the man.

Frank Pittman

Being a father is certainly a task. But the best one that I could ever ask for.

Chris Hemsworth

OUT OF ALL THE DADS IN THE WORLD, I'M PRETTY SURE I GOT THE BEST ONE

My kids are my number one priority no matter what I'm doing.

Lin-Manuel Miranda

Men should always change diapers. It's a very rewarding experience. It's mentally cleansing.

Chris Martin

WHEN YOU
ARE BY MY
SIDE, I FEEL
AS THOUGH
I CAN DO
ANYTHING

**Dads are
stone skimmers,
mud wallowers,
water wallopers,
ceiling swoopers,
shoulder gallopers,
upsy-downsy,
over-and-through,
round-and-about
whooshers.**

Helen Thomson

Fatherhood will put a man through a lot, but it's a tremendous job, the best in the world.

Derek Fisher

The hardest part of my new life as a dad is leaving for work in the morning.

Mario Lopez

THANK YOU FOR BEING MY FIRST AND BEST TEACHER

Anyone who tells you fatherhood is the greatest thing that can happen to you, they are understating it.

Mike Myers

Lately all my
friends are
worried they're
turning into
their fathers.
I'm worried
I'm not.

Dan Zevin

YOU ARE MY COMPASS – THANKS FOR ALWAYS GUIDING ME TO THE RIGHT PATH

To me as a
new father,
nothing is
more important
or scary than
protecting
a daughter.

Channing Tatum

When you have kids, there's no such thing as quality time. There's just time.

Chris Rock

Fathers
like mine
don't ever die.

Leo Buscaglia

I
APPRECIATE
YOU MORE
EVERY DAY

Allow your daughter or your son to know that they can come to you for anything.

Jamie Foxx

When a father gives to his son, both laugh; when a son gives to his father, both cry.

William Shakespeare

YOU
TAUGHT ME
WHAT LOVE
REALLY IS

Are we not
like two volumes
of one book?

Marceline
Desbordes-Valmore

What I learned
most from my
father wasn't
anything he said;
it was just the way
he behaved.

Jeff Bridges

EVERY SON'S FIRST SUPERHERO IS HIS FATHER.

Tiger Shroff

YOU ARE A PATIENT TEACHER, AN AMAZING PERSON, AND A WONDERFUL FATHER

I truly – every single night – say, "I can't believe these two amazing girls are mine."

John Krasinski

**To be the father
of a nation is
a great honour,
but to be the
father of a family
is a greater joy.**

Nelson Mandela

YOU WILL ALWAYS BE MY NUMBER ONE

The raising
of a child is
the building of
a cathedral.
You can't cut
corners.

Dave Eggers

Having a child lifts you out of selfish behaviour and gives you responsibility... I take great pride in being a father.

Tom Hardy

My dad believed in me even when I didn't.

Taylor Swift

THANK YOU FOR ALWAYS TEACHING ME TO FOLLOW MY OWN STAR

**A father is
the one friend
upon whom we
can always rely.**

Émile Gaboriau

You get into your house and shut the door and it's lovely to be greeted by this person who's become the most important thing.

James Corden
on his son

I LOVE SPENDING TIME WITH YOU

Any man can be a father, but it takes someone special to be a dad.

Anonymous

My father gave me
the greatest gift
anyone could give
another person: he
believed in me.

Jim Valvano

I want it to be the greatest thing I ever do: make good humans.

Jason Momoa

I HOPE
YOU KNOW
JUST HOW
GREATLY
I ADMIRE
YOU

I LOVE FATHERHOOD. I COULD BANG ON ABOUT KIDS FOREVER.

Guy Ritchie

One father
is more than
a hundred
schoolmasters.

George Herbert

YOU MADE GROWING UP FUN

I have found the best way to give advice to your children is to find out what they want and then advise them to do it.

Harry S. Truman

Of all the titles I've been privileged to have, "Dad" has been always the best.

Ken Norton

I think my mom
put it best. She said,
"Little girls soften
their daddies' hearts."

Paul Walker

WHEN I NEED ADVICE OR WISDOM, YOU ARE THE FIRST PERSON I TURN TO

When my father didn't have my hand, he had my back.

Linda Poindexter

My father... taught me to work hard, laugh often, and keep my word.

Michelle Obama

AS TIME
GOES ON WE
ONLY GROW
CLOSER
AND
CLOSER

My father gave
me my dreams.
Thanks to him,
I could see
a future.

Liza Minnelli

Everything just gets heightened when you have a baby. The volume gets turned up on life.

Jimmy Fallon

Never is a man more of a man than when he is the father of a newborn.

Matthew McConaughey

YOU ARE SUCH A STRONG EXAMPLE TO ME IN EVERYTHING YOU DO

It's amazing that you can be that exhausted and that happy at the same time.

Ryan Reynolds
on raising children

The sooner you treat your son as a man, the sooner he will be one.

John Dryden

WHEN THINGS ARE TOUGH, YOU HELP ME FIND THE STRENGTH TO CONTINUE

What we become
depends on what our
fathers teach us at
odd moments, when
they aren't trying
to teach us.

Umberto Eco

Being present with your child: that's the greatest gift that you can give.

David Beckham

My daddy's everything. I hope I can find a man that will treat me as good as my dad.

Lady Gaga

I AM WHERE
I AM TODAY
BECAUSE YOU
LISTENED,
ENCOURAGED,
AND BELIEVED

I've gotten to jump out of helicopters and do daring stunts... but none of them mean anything compared to being somebody's daddy.

Chris Pratt

Having a baby – it's massive. Suddenly I understood my parents much more proudly than I ever had before.

Benedict Cumberbatch

YOU'VE GIVEN ME EVERYTHING I EVER NEEDED, AND A LOT MORE BESIDES

**The heart of
a father is the
masterpiece
of nature.**

Antoine François Prévost

It's a very powerful feeling to see the product of your love right there in front of you.

John Legend
on his children

**Fatherly love
is the ability to
expect the best
from your children
despite the facts.**

Jasmine Birtles

I COULDN'T
ASK FOR A
BETTER ROLE
MODEL THAN
YOU

My father didn't tell me how to live. He lived and let me watch him do it.

Clarence Budington Kelland

Fatherhood is
a very natural
thing; it's not
something that
shakes up my
life but rather
it enriches it.

Andrea Bocelli

YOU KNOW ME BETTER THAN ANYONE

Being a father is such a trip... an amazing discovery every day.

Justin Timberlake

Being a father is the greatest job I have ever had and the greatest job I will ever have.

Dwayne Johnson

The mark of
a good parent
is that he can
have fun while
being one.

Marcelene Cox

I WOULD NOT BE NOT BE WHO I AM TODAY WITHOUT YOU

My father was my teacher. But most importantly he was a great dad.

Beau Bridges

When you have kids, you see life through different eyes.

Dave Grohl

I CAN ALWAYS FACE WHATEVER'S IN FRONT OF ME KNOWING YOU HAVE MY BACK

Love isn't enough
despite what every
sappy love song
says; commitment
to parenting was
the missing piece.
Commitment takes
love on its back
and carries it
the whole way.

Terry Crews

My father didn't do anything unusual. He only did what dads are supposed to do – be there.

Max Lucado

IT IS A WISE FATHER THAT KNOWS HIS OWN CHILD.

William Shakespeare

WHEN SOMETHING AMAZING HAPPENS, YOU ARE ALWAYS THE FIRST PERSON I NEED TO TELL

I don't mind
looking into
the mirror and
seeing my father.

Michael Douglas

He was a father.
That's what a
father does.
Eases the
burdens of
those he loves.

George Saunders

I'M SO GRATEFUL FOR EVERYTHING YOU'VE DONE FOR ME

I didn't even know
that there was
that colour in the
spectrum. I didn't
know that level of
love existed.

Michael Bublé
on fatherhood

There is more
to fathers than
meets the eye.

Margaret Atwood

I'm a father;
that's what
matters most.
Nothing
matters more.

Gordon Brown

WHO NEEDS SUPERHEROES WHEN I HAVE YOU?

It's the courage
to raise a child
that makes you
a father.

Barack Obama

**Every day
I'm proud
to be a dad.
Every morning.
Every evening.**

Chris Rock

YOU
BRING OUT
THE BEST
IN ME

To her, the name of father was another name for love.

Fanny Fern

I always knew one
day fatherhood
would be great,
I just didn't
think it would
be this great.

Marquise Goodwin

It's just lovely to have all that love around. Suddenly you love someone more than yourself.

Hugh Grant

FIRST MY FATHER, FOREVER MY FRIEND

The love I have
for my wife is
so intense, but
nothing prepared
me for the love I
have for my kids.

Hugh Jackman

Life doesn't
come with an
instruction book.
That's why we
have fathers.

H. Jackson Brown Jr

I HAVE
SO MANY
HAPPY
MEMORIES
WITH YOU

MY DAD TAUGHT ME THAT GOOD HEALTH IS ALL ABOUT LIVING IN GRATITUDE.

Mariska Hargitay

**My dad's
my best mate,
and he always
will be.**

Cher Lloyd

It is not flesh and blood, but heart which makes us fathers and sons.

Johann Friedrich von Schiller

YOU TAUGHT ME HOW TO FIND THE POSSIBLE IN THE IMPOSSIBLE

All the things you hear about going into parenting are true. I've never known love like this.

Matthew Morrison

To me, having kids is the ultimate job in life. I want to be most successful at being a good father.

Nick Lachey

**FIRST I
GOT TO SIT
ON YOUR
SHOULDER;
NOW I GET
TO LEAN
ON IT**

The biggest lesson
for my kids is that
they know they are
the most important
things I have.

Lin-Manuel Miranda

Having a
family makes
whatever
other thing you
have that
much richer.

Ben Affleck

THE MOST IMPORTANT THING IN THE WORLD IS FAMILY AND LOVE.

John Wooden

EVERY
TIME I SAY
SOMETHING
WISE I ADD,
"MY DAD
TOLD ME
THAT"

The family is one of nature's masterpieces.

George Santayana

Success, and
even life itself,
wouldn't be worth
anything if I didn't
have... my children
by my side.

Jude Law

THANK YOU FOR ALL THE TIMES YOU PUT ME FIRST

Having a kid
is like falling
in love for the
first time when
you're 12 but
every day.

Mike Myers

There's the idea
that we as parents
spend all this
time protecting
our children.
No, I think they're
protecting us.

Chris Hemsworth

There's no pillow quite so soft as a father's strong shoulder.

Richard L. Evans

YOU ALWAYS
KNOW WHEN
TO BE A
PARENT,
WHEN TO
BE A GUIDE,
AND WHEN
TO BE A
FRIEND

Noble fathers
have noble
children.

Euripides

Fatherhood is the best thing that could happen to me, and I'm just glad I can share my voice.

Dwayne Wade

YOU MEAN THE ABSOLUTE WORLD TO ME

No man stands
so tall as when
he stoops to
help a child.

Anonymous

Blessed indeed is the man who hears many gentle voices call him father.

Lydia Maria Child

I think the whole thing about fatherhood is the surprises don't stop.

Sam Wood

YOU REALLY ARE THE BEST DAD EVER

I haven't taught people in 50 years what my father taught by example in one week.

Mario Cuomo

With them,
my dreams finally
came true. I'm a
father. I found my
place, my home.

Jason Momoa

Have you enjoyed this book?
If so, find us on Facebook at
Summersdale Publishers, on Twitter
at **@Summersdale** and on Instagram
at **@summersdalebooks** and get in
touch. We'd love to hear from you!

www.summersdale.com